Working From Home In 2020

Making The New Ways To Promote Your Work

Copyright © 2021

All rights reserved.

DEDICATION

The author and publisher have provided this e-book to you for your personal use only. You may not make this e-book publicly available in any way. Copyright infringement is against the law. If you believe the copy of this e-book you are reading infringes on the author's copyright, please notify the publisher at: https://us.macmillan.com/piracy

Contents

What Is A Remote Job? 1
    Are Remote Jobs Freelance or Employee Jobs? 1

Best Remote Jobs and Careers for Remote Workers 3
    1. Developer 3
    2. Online Marketing 4
    3. Designer 5
    4. Writer/Editor 6
    5. Customer Support 7
    6. Teacher 8
    7. Accountant 10
    8. Data Entry 11
    9. Virtual Assistant 12
    10. Social Media Manager 13

6 Steps How to Get a Remote Job This Weekend 15
    1. Ask Yourself if Getting a Remote Job is Actually Right for You 15
    2. Determine What Really Motivates You at Work 19
    3. How to Find Your Dream Remote Job 20
    4. Know What Remote Employers Are Looking For 33
    5. Crafting a Resume for a Remote Job Application 36
    6. Bringing it All Home (No Pun Intended) 39

How to Be A Happy and Successful Remote Worker? 42

What Is A Remote Job?

A remote job is one that is done away from the office in a remote location. This could be either work done from home, or work done on the road in the case of a job such as a Regional Salesperson.

Are Remote Jobs Freelance or Employee Jobs?

The answer here is also a bit of both. Remote jobs can be employee-based jobs or freelance jobs, depending on how each individual employer sets up the role. This is usually spelled out clearly in the job description, but if it's not clear, make a note to ask the company during the interview process.

We hope this gives you some insight into why job descriptions choose one of these phrases over the others.

However, because they are often used interchangeably, it's important to read the job description carefully to get a better sense of exactly what a company means when it uses phrases like remote job, telework, telecommuting, home-based job, or virtual job.

Best Remote Jobs and Careers for Remote Workers

1. Developer

Being a "developer" is a blanket term for a huge variety of tech-friendly jobs. This category can include anything from software engineering, to app development, to website design, systems administration, testing, and ops infrastructure.

Bottom line:

It's one of the most popular categories for a reason—there's demand, and it pays. The tech industry is the future of how we work, so it's no surprise that many location-free jobs fall within this category. It's a great option for those who love to travel, too, because it's often self-paced work that is low-client facing.

If you don't have experience with web development, don't worry. There are many resources out there to help you get started at any skill level. It may go without saying, but this career is best suited for the tech-savvy.

2. Online Marketing

Online marketing is another popular and varied career option for digital nomads. Within this category are jobs related to SEO and PPC, traffic generation, affiliated marketing, and inbound marketing.

Bottom line:

With a low barrier to entry and high demand, these jobs are great for generalist nomads. Almost every company has a website that needs marketing, every successful blog has well-planned SEO strategies, and inbound marketing, which is increasing in popularity, requires thoughtful content creation. These jobs aren't hard to come by, and it doesn't take too long to master the skills.

There are many resources out there to help you learn the basics of any of these types of marketing, many of which are free. It's also important to start a blog and ramp up your social media presence to show employers your skills.

3. Designer

For the more creative digital nomads, web-based design may be a viable option. Graphic design, WordPress theme design, UX and UI design all fall within this category and all require different skill sets.

Bottom line:

With tons of free and paid resources out there, it's not impossible to break into the web-design field. Though many stable jobs require experience, freelance is a reliable place to start. Additionally, this is another job with high demand and a bright future—everybody with a product to sell, business to maintain, or presence to grow needs design help. Plus, travel can be a WAY better inspiration than an office cubicle!

4. Writer/Editor

Blog writing is a popular way to start, especially for those who love to travel and write about their experiences. Beyond blogging, though, is a whole world of writing and editing opportunities.

Technical writing is a well-paid niche for those who have knowledge in a specific field—manuals, online help articles, training, and reports all fall within this category.

Copywriting is a type of persuasive writing, great for those with a marketing mindset.

For those who love to write, eBook self-publishing is a good way to earn passive income once the work is put in. With sites like Amazon and E-junkie, it's never been easier to get your writing out there.

You can also make extra money with your writing by building SEO backlinks. SEO is a $75 billion industry and backlinks are very valuable for any online business. Many SEO agencies work with freelance writers to help them build backlinks for their clients. You can also find link building jobs directly yourself by utilizing Link-able, a quality marketplace site that connects businesses with freelance authors who can build great backlinks.

Bottom line:

Flexibility and buildable skills define this job. Once you've got a portfolio built, it's easy to score well-paid freelance jobs on any one of the many, many freelance sites out there.

5. Customer Support

Location independent customer support careers are another expanding field. All it takes to be successful in this career is a computer with wifi, call or chat software, and great customer services skills. Even more opportunities are available to those with specialized skills.

Bottom line:

Customer support jobs require little contact with the rest of the team, and many companies know this and are willing to hire distance-based employees. Usually companies look for impeccable English skills, the ability to work autonomously, and mastery of simple admin tasks like tracking data on Excel.

This job is great for remote workers because of the flexibility. There are a huge number of industries that need customer support, and sometimes being in a different timezone from the customers is a benefit (hello would-be night shift turned day shift!). Plus, the pay is surprisingly reasonable with Glassdoor quoting most earning somewhere around $30,000 annually.

6. Teacher

Teaching English is a pretty common way to satisfy your travel bug while making cash. But with the ever-increasing presence of the internet, a whole new world of teaching has opened up. No longer are you confined to the classroom, or even one location! Online tutoring, teaching, curriculum building, and course building are all options for digital nomads.

Nikki J. is a long-time digital nomad currently living in Japan, although she has also lived in Vietnam, Argentina, and France, to name a few. Nikki earns a living by teaching and tutoring languages online– she speaks English, French, and Spanish, and hosts her lessons on Skype and says, "It's actually very easy to build a customer base. There are so many platforms out there for language teachers. And a plethora of teaching resources out there. So, it's not even that difficult to make lesson plans!" Nikki also commented that she loves her job and how it allows her to connect with people from all around the world wherever she's at.

Bottom line:

This is another job with great flexibility and numerous opportunities. Teaching and tutoring are not just confined to English. Chemistry, music, math, literature… if you had a favourite subject in school, odds are you can teach or tutor it online! Many teachers and tutors find work through agencies that match them and it just takes a quick Google search to find hundreds.

Another viable career path is in curriculum or course creation. The type of work can range anywhere from freelance writing a college curriculum, to learning how to and building your own courses online. For example, many people build courses on, essentially, how to do whatever it is you do! And once all the work is done and you've hosted your course on a site like Wyzant or Skooli, it's a way to earn passive income.

7. Accountant

Accounting jobs may seem like pretty boring desk jobs to some, but in reality much of the work of an accountant can be done from just about anywhere on a computer in the right industries. This is especially true for niche areas, like international tax preparation, small business accounting, and so on.

Bottom line:

This career is great for nomads who want to stick with more traditional jobs while still living out their travel dreams. More and more opportunities are likely to open up as businesses continue to adapt to new technologies. Additionally, it's also possible to market yourself to fellow digital nomads who are looking to get their own businesses, or personal, finances in order!

Please note that to be an accountant, usually a bachelor's degree and certification is required.

8. Data Entry

Why it's great: Data entry is in high-demand and can pretty much be done anywhere, anytime, which is great news for nomads! Data is integral to business– it's used to help the tracking of inventory and shipments, used to aid in business plan creation, and can assist businesses in measuring performance and output.

Bottom line:

Although it's beneficial to have some previous experience, this is reflected in the relatively stable compensation. There are freelance, one-time gig, opportunities out there, too, though, so if you need to brush up on your data entry skills, it's not impossible to get started while already on the road. This is an especially great job for the tech and business savvy nomads out there.

9. Virtual Assistant

These days many small businesses outsource tedious tasks to virtual assistants. There's a lot that goes into running a business, much of which can be done from anywhere with internet access! The type of work ranges anywhere from secretarial duties, like handling appointments, to more technical work, like updating websites.

Kelsey D., a digital nomad who travels the backroads of the United States every chance she gets, works as a virtual assistant for a small shoe design company based in Chicago. Kelsey manages appointment calendars, conference call note taking, inventory and shipment databases, and answering client emails. When asked how she came across this job, she said, "It was really the perfect fit for me. I love fashion and design, but needed something flexible to fit my lifestyle and allowed me to work while on the road. I actually found this company while looking for jobs on Craigslist, bought a pocket wifi, and have never looked back."

Bottom line:

If you're an especially organized nomad, this job might be for you! Depending on your skill set or niche, there's a huge market for virtual assistants. These jobs can range anywhere from short-term contracts, one-time gigs, to long-term partnerships or permanent employment.

10. Social Media Manager

This is a newer job that has been seeing huge growth within the last couple of years, and is great for those who love social media. Being a Social Media Manager means looking after the various social media accounts that most companies seem to have today. Duties could include making posts, answering inquiries, planning out strategies for user involvement, and so on. These days a great number of companies have this position, or one like it, or even hire freelance managers to help them out.

Bottom line:

Although it's a relatively new job, there are thousands of listings on sites like careerbuilder.com, simplyhired.com, and upwork.com. Often some experience is required, but this experience can be gained by building your own social media presence, or helping out those in your network. Often times Social Media Managers are paid by the hour, or with a monthly or retainer fee.

Check out some of the following resources for more information, job listings, or course listings! With a new year, comes new and better technology. The future of location-independent careers is bright, so these are just a few of the options out there. Take some time to research if you're thinking of making the transition into the digital nomad life, but be assured that it's very possible to do what you love while also living how you want.

6 Steps How to Get a Remote Job This Weekend

1. Ask Yourself if Getting a Remote Job is Actually Right for You

Before we get entrenched in actually landing a remote job, we need to talk about whether or not remote is right for you specifically. This part requires some research and self-reflection.

For example, remote work is an awesome fit for my personal lifestyle and work style, for the following reasons:
- I'm extroverted, but I get a lot of in-person interaction from friends outside of work.
- I love talking to people. Talking on the phone or via video chat satisfies my need for in-person communication just as much as actual, in-person communication.
- I'm also a big runner, and I love spending time with my family.
- I love my work, I have no problem focusing, and I'm able to tear myself away from work when I'm done for the day.

If you want to jump into remote work with both feet, it's really important to ask yourself if the pros outweigh the cons. For me, there was major upside, and it was a no brainer to go remote and take on work from home jobs. For you the story might be different.

We've listed off the pros and cons to working from home below. Look at them through the lens of your own ideal lifestyle, and the lens of what makes you most productive.

Pros of Getting a Remote Job:
1. **No commute:** your once dreaded commute is over, no more traffic or annoying rush hour subway rides
2. **Your own schedule:** Nobody is watching. Want to watch Netflix at 11:00 a.m. on a Monday? Go ahead, no one will know. Depending on your job function, you can work when you want to.
3. **Work anywhere:** you can work literally anywhere. I work on my back deck when it's nice out, but some people choose to work in a different country every few months.
4. **Family time:** If you have kids (or a pair of Cavalier King Charles Spaniels) you'll have more time to hang with them. Obviously, you

don't want them to invade your workspace, but work flexibility allows for more family (or dog) time.

5. **Costs:** Commute costs are nil. You can also say goodbye to $13 salads for lunch and say hello to the supermarket for a cheaper breakfast and lunch.
6. **Office stress and distractions:** No one is stopping by your desk and distracting you from work. No office drama with remote work.

Sounds great right? Not so fast, there are some downsides to working remotely:

Cons of Getting a Remote Job:

1. **Loneliness:** I once had somebody tell me that "working at home alone is a good way toward sadness". I actually agree. Working 5 days per week completely alone can get lonely.
2. **Overworking:** Seems like underworking would be the problem here…right? In reality, more people struggle to divide home life and work life, resulting in a never ending work day. Burnout becomes very real, very fast, if you fall into bad work habits at home.

3. **Underworking:** Depending on your personality, overall work ethic, and love for your job function, productivity can actually drop in a remote environment. If direct supervision motivates you to get work done, working from home might kill your motivation.
4. **No "water cooler moments":** Some say that creativity and innovation can happen at impromptu moments at work. Being physically close to coworkers creates more interpersonal communication. Some of these moments are lost with remote work.
5. **Limited team social activities:** Some companies are partly remote. For example, maybe only 10% of the workforce is remote. When everyone goes out for a happy hour, you and the other remote team members might be too far away to join. feelings of seclusion ensue.

Remote work is not for everybody, some people really thrive in an office environment, and others thrive working remotely.

I've talked to some people that tried out remote work and quickly realized that they need more in-person interaction. I've talked to other people that ended up back in the office because they simply want someplace to go every day.

Now that you know the pros and cons of having a remote job, it's time to do some self-reflection.

2. Determine What Really Motivates You at Work

Taking a remote job is almost like being an entrepreneur, and motivational quotes alone won't fuel you forever.

No one is over your shoulder telling you to do your job. With remote work, the only person telling you to work is you.

The best remote workers really love their work and take pride in what they produce. If you don't love what you do, your bed suddenly becomes really comfortable — especially when no one is telling you to get up and go.

Most people start to get this feeling of dread on Sunday nights for one reason or another. If you get that feeling, analyze it. If you hate being in customer success at the office, you'll probably hate being in customer success at home too. If you like your job but the Sunday dread comes from the stress of commuting, you might be a good fit for remote work.

I personally look forward to Mondays (honestly) because I really like what I do, and I get to do what I love from home.

Having a remote job is an amazing opportunity to live the lifestyle that you want while doing the work that you love. Just make sure it's a fit for you personally before hitting the remote job boards.

3. How to Find Your Dream Remote Job

If you're still reading, you're probably ready to storm the virtual gates of the remote work-world. Still, if you want to get a remote job… you'll first need to know where to look.

The Best Sites for Finding Great Remote Jobs

Most job sites don't have a very good "remote work" filter, which usually results in hours of sifting through freelance jobs and other gigs that might not be the best fit. All of the job boards below do the sifting for you and feature specifically remote jobs:

In my experience, these are hands down the 6 best sites for finding remote jobs:

1. FlexJobs

This site offers full-time, part-time, and even some jobs that are perfect for testing your way into starting a freelance business. Companies can post jobs for free, but candidates have to pay $14.99 a month for the service. Frankly, the $14.99 is a small price to pay for access to the job opportunities they post. I personally know a few people that have landed a position through Flexjobs.

Outside of the paid service, they also have a ton of free resources for remote job seekers. Most of the other sites I will talk about feature "jobs in tech", but Flexjobs offers job postings from a wide variety of industries. Bonus: Flexjobs has new posts all the time, and posters usually get back to you quickly after you've applied.

2. AngelList

I've personally gotten a job from AngelList. There's no fee and new job postings are added daily. Unlike the other sites on this list, this site is geared specifically toward start-ups. If you want to work at an early stage startup, this is the place to be. There is no cost to use AngelList, but you'll need to make

a profile. Your profile is your resume so make sure it stands out. You get interviews by clicking "yes, I'm interested" and by leaving a small note for the hiring manager. If the company likes your profile, they will set up a meeting with you. The process with AngelList is super easy, no resume or cover letter needed. I've applied and received a response within a few hours, and each job posting tells you when the job poster was last "active". Pro Tip: stay away from the "active 2 months ago," or later.

3. Hubstaff Talent

On Hubstaff, you have the option of searching for remote jobs that are full-time, hourly freelance contract, and even fixed price—so this platform is particularly great if you're looking to take on freelance work to supplement your income. With their hundreds of open roles ranging from web development, to design, marketing, sales, customer service, social media marketing and more, there's something for everyone on this remote job platform.

4. Pangian

When you join Pangian, you're tapping into one of the fastest-growing online communities for not only finding remote jobs, but for connecting with fellow remote workers that are based in more than 121 countries from around the world. While their remote job board currently boasts over 12,897 jobs from 312 companies, the platform's real magic lies within their close-knit community and chat forums where you can swap remote working tips & learn from one another.

5. Remote.com

This site gives you access to a range of start-ups to publicly traded companies. Job seekers can apply for free when their profile matches the requirements for a job. Remote.com also has a $19 premium option for additional exposure. Check out their "companies" page and you'll see some big names. If you decide to sign up for Remote.com they'll let you see the compensation for jobs before you apply to them.

I also really like Remote.com because they post so many jobs. If you check every day, they'll usually put up 4-5 jobs from at least 1 new company. Remote.com posts get good response times, most will respond within a day or two.

6.   **Remote.co**

Remote.co (not remote.com) is actually part of Flexjobs, but offers some additional job postings. I'm putting this site on the list because of the resources. They post jobs daily (and good jobs at that), and their "companies" page is an amazing place to learn about companies that hire remote workers.

If you do end up applying for a job, the response time is similar to that of a regular job application. They have great blog resources and an FAQ section for remote job seekers. The job posting quality is good, but again, this is a great place to learn about working remotely.

7.   **WeWorkRemotely**

This is almost purely a job board, but a great job board for remote jobs. There is no application fee, and the site is really easy to navigate. One downside here is slower application response times (not sure why).

Most of the jobs are focused on software engineering/ design, but this is a daily-checker if you are on the remote job hunt. When I'm looking for a remote job, I make sure to check WeWorkRemotely for sure.

8.   Jobspresso

This site is another "check everyday" job board. They have postings from some of the biggest names in remote work, and they post new jobs every day. I like Jobspresso because they have a high volume of jobs, and they post often. Not a whole lot of job seeking resources here, but following them on Twitter is a really nice way to keep up with postings.

Having looked for remote jobs in the not so distant past, those sites have yielded some great opportunities. I've had great experiences with the above companies, but I can't say the same for the websites below. Here are some sites that are NOT good for remote work:

The Worst Sites for Finding Remote Jobs

1.   **LinkedIn.**

Maybe a surprise? Linkedin is the biggest professional network and arguably the best place to find a job… but it's not the best place to find a remote job. I'll give them some credit: they have been adding more remote jobs lately. But in general, remote jobs are hard to find, and they often end up being in-person jobs.

Looking for an in-person job? Linkedin is your best bet. But remote? You'll be sifting through jobs for hours—and when you finally find the needle-in-the-haystack remote job, the job poster has usually made a mistake. You'll find the job is not remote or the company is not very desirable. If you have unlimited hours for job seeking, you might find a few remote jobs in here, but those same jobs are usually posted on one of the recommended remote job boards.

2. Indeed

My beef here is mainly around wasted time. There are actually a fair amount of remote jobs on Indeed, and they are easy to find, but a lot of them are location specific or not remote at all. The remote companies on Indeed can be suspect at times too. If you are looking for a remote job in tech, this is not the place to look.

But, I will say that Indeed does offer remote jobs in industries outside of technology. For my intended job search (I've worked in tech), this place was a dud. If I was looking for a job outside of tech, maybe not. Overall though—the postings here are peppered with weird companies and non-remote jobs, cloaked as remote jobs. Thus my badge of disapproval.

3. Monster

This is just straight up not the place for remote jobs. I don't think they focus on it, and it shows. They rarely post remote jobs, and when they do, the jobs are usually location specific or with an unknown company. I think Monster is a good place to find a non-remote job, but it's not worth your time to search here for remote openings.

Depending on your skill set and industry experience, one of the recommended remote job boards might be more valuable than the others. For me specifically, AngelList was hugely helpful. I used it to find a job at a small tech startup in a sales capacity. If I had a different job function or different industry experience, I might start with Flexjobs. They have great tech openings, but they also service an array of industries.

There are other remote job sites, but no matter what industry or job function you're looking for, the 6 mentioned above are the best places to start.

Know the Key Players Who Hire Remote Employees

Once you've been poking around the remote job sites, you'll start to see some familiar company names and familiar thought leaders within remote work.

The first step in the remote community: understanding the differences between fully and partially distributed companies.

Distributed is just a word describing companies that don't have an office. Hence, a fully distributed company is where everyone in the company works remotely. Some people might share a workspace if they live in the same city — But for the most part, everyone works from different places.

Partially distributed companies are any company with 1 or more remote workers. These companies might describe themselves as "remote friendly" or "remote flexible".

Know the Difference Between Partially vs. Fully Distributed Remote Teams

As an applicant, it doesn't matter if the company is fully or partially distributed, because who cares, if the position is remote.

It doesn't matter if everyone else works in an office… right?

Actually, it really does matter

Most fully distributed companies started fully distributed, and they have solid onboarding systems (and ongoing training programs) to show for it.
Partially distributed companies sometimes struggle with transitioning from a centralized workforce, to a remote workforce. "Sometimes" is the operative word though.

There are many partially distributed companies that have successfully integrated a remote workforce. You may want to ask about remote onboarding in the interview process. If the company indicates that their remote onboarding process is air-tight, you'll be set up for success.

For example, I worked for a company where I was the only remote employee, and onboarding was non-existent. Unfortunately, I forgot to ask about onboarding as a remote employee, and I ended up paying for it, I didn't hit my goals as fast as I should have.

To be clear, I'm not saying that fully distributed is better than partially distributed. Most remote companies will offer an amazing onboarding and work experience, regardless of whether or not they are fully or partially distributed. That said, it can't hurt to ask about how dedicated the company is to remote work, and about the systems they've set up for remote workers.

It also can't hurt to do some homework on remote.
I would highly suggest reading some of those Q&A's. You'll get insights into how remote companies work, how they started, where their HQ is (if they have one), and the breakdown of remote vs. non-remote employees. Big hint: most of the interviews are with HR directors and VPs of HR— great people to reach out to if you're serious about a specific company.

Knowing the remote community is a huge step towards getting a remote job. Most people give up because remote companies are hard to find. So clap it up, at this point you're a remote job market hacker!

But let's get back to serious stuff for a minute. There are only a few companies offering remote positions, relative to the overall job market. You need to be able to find those positions and get to them quickly. Knowing the right job site is the finding part, and social media is the way to learn about postings quickly.

Remember those companies on the top 100 list and Q&A list? Follow them on social media. I follow almost all of them on Twitter, and they are constantly posting jobs. Checking the job boards works really well, but as soon as the company posts a job, they'll post it on social media too.

If you still have any skepticism about working remotely, remote companies usually produce tons of content around remote work. For example, Trello posts on their blog weekly and some of their content is focused around working remotely. You'll get really good insight into remote work culture by just following remote company blogs and social media.

Half the battle to landing a remote job is knowing where to look, and knowing the community of remote companies, but that's still not going to land you a job. Remote companies are very careful about who they hire, and they're looking for some pretty specific attributes.

4. Know What Remote Employers Are Looking For

The majority of remote employers are looking for two main things: (1) trustworthy people and (2) those that actually love their work.

I say trustable because micromanagement is death for remote companies. Remote employers need to trust that each team member will do their job, and create high-quality work.
When you land your first remote interview, don't be surprised if your interviewer seems to be really interested to talk about you as a person. Diversity is valued. You might be communicating with team members in San Francisco, Bombay, London, and Mexico City in the same day. If you spend time working on a personal blog, or like to travel and kitesurf on weekends, don't hold that information back either. In a remote interview, don't be afraid to be you. Side note: If you want to build your skills as a blogger, start with these blogging courses from the world's top experts today.

I hate when people tell me to "just be yourself"—But in remote interviews, dialing back the corporate speak and acting like yourself makes you more trustworthy. I've noticed that a lot of remote workers (remote hiring managers) seem to, for some reason, have higher emotional intelligence than usual. They'll be able to tell if you are being genuine.

I talked about self-reflection a little earlier: here comes some more internal pondering.

Outside of hiring trustable people, remote companies want people that are passionate about what they do.
If you are getting a remote job just because you hate your work, and you're hoping that working from home will help…unfortunately, it won't. Working from home might even make it worse.

Working from home offers myriad wonderful distractions. Your TV might be calling your name at lunch, and your dog might be calling your name all day. If you're not motivated to work, you likely won't work if no one is looking over your shoulder.
Remote work is reserved for people that love, or at least really like what they are doing. Sounds harsh, but your motivators need to be in the right place. If you show your remote interviewer how much you actually care about your work, I promise, it will resonate with them.

To recap: be genuine and show passion for your work (one way to demonstrate that interest is to start a blog, share clever blog post ideas in your field and eventually even make money blogging). Now that you are ready to nail the soft skills portion of the interview, some hard skills are necessary for working remotely:

Remote companies are looking for problem solvers. This might come in the form of start-up experience, entrepreneurial experience, internally innovative people (intrapreneurs), or just plain other remote work experience.

Why do they want this experience? Because there will come a time where you'll have a question, and your entire company might be unavailable. They'll want you to be versatile, and capable of solving problems on your own.

When I worked in an office, my boss was in the cubicle across from me. If there was an emergency, I could just run over to her and say, HELP!

To be clear, Slack and other communication tools exist for a reason. You probably won't be left to the wolves often. But remote companies are looking for autonomous workers. In the interview process, be ready to speak about your autonomous work experience.

Don't think you have autonomous work experience? Don't worry, nobody really does… unless you've worked remotely or started your own business before. Time to get creative.

I started an e-commerce company as a side hustle few years ago. I worked on it when I got home from my day job. I also had a painting company in college where I went door to door selling painting services. All of that shows my self-starter experience.

5. Crafting a Resume for a Remote Job Application.

Self-starter experience goes a long way in an interview. But to land an interview, your resume needs to be tailored to remote companies. Here are a few things to put on your resume that'll make it stand out to remote employers (and one extremely useful resume builder to check out):

Talk about tools: Remote companies use software to bridge the communication gap. List any software tools that you are familiar with using. Some might include: Slack, Salesforce, Basecamp, Trello, Harvest, GoToMeeting, Google Hangouts, Skype, Zoom, Zapier, and many more.

Communication: Communication starts with your resume. Remote companies fail because of bad communication, thus they look to hire amazing communicators. Your resume should talk about your communication skills, and typos should be non-existent. Your email communication with hiring managers and recruiters should be great too, and it can't hurt to mention that you'll take your cybersecurity seriously as a remote employee too.

Innovation or portfolio: If you have done something to innovate at work, put that on your resume. If you have a portfolio, share that too.

Side projects: Depending upon how you breach this subject, side projects can start some controversy. You might not want to put those projects front and center on your resume unless it adds to your case, but you'll want to talk about them in an interview. Working on a project autonomously shows that you take initiative. I say tread lightly because some employers, remote or not, might think that your side project is going to take time away from your day job.

Location: This may seem obvious, but if a remote job is location specific, make sure to mention your proximity to that location. For example, some sales jobs might have an NYC territory. If you live in NYC, make sure that you mention it in your correspondence with the company.

Results: If you have any hard numbers associated with your job, put those on the resume too. For example, if you have the marketing skills and you doubled traffic in X period of time, due to X reasons – that's good resume information.

Autonomy: Can't hurt to talk about any time you were a "self-starter" or worked on deliverables without much supervision. Any time you worked with low or no supervision is valuable. Your ability to work autonomously is big, but you don't need to have direct remote experience to work remotely.

Working remotely is much more results focused than hours-worked focused. Some remote positions will require 9:00-5:00 work hours, but others won't at all. Some remote companies won't monitor your hours worked, but they'll be monitoring your deliverables.

If you love your work, you're a genuine person, and you tailor your resume to remote companies. You're on the right track to landing a remote job.

6. Bringing it All Home (No Pun Intended)

One last tip before you hit the remote job boards: pick up a copy of Remote by Jason Fried and David Heinemeier Hansson (founders of Basecamp). I promise that no one from Basecamp forced me to talk about their business book (nor did they pay me off), I just found the book to provide great insights into working remotely.

For remote job seekers, the book outlines how a good remote company is managed and provides you with an outline of what to look for in a remote employer.

With your reading list in hand, here's a recap of your action items for getting a remote job:

- Determine if remote is right for you personally (maybe you'd be happy where you are with a raise?).
- Weigh the pros and cons, and know your own motivators.
- Know the right sites for remote job hunting.
- Know the worst sites for remote job hunting.
- Get familiar with the remote community.
- Be trustable, be autonomous, and love your work.
- Tailor your resume for remote job applications.
- Take your job search into your own hands.

When you do finally get a remote job, it might seem weird at first… working for a company with no HQ, or a company with an HQ thousands of miles away. Give it a few weeks and you'll feel right at home (literally).

Honestly, on my first day of remote work, while I was waiting to meet my new manager on our conference line, it crossed my mind that the whole company might not even be real.

I had this flash of worry that the whole thing was fake! Then the meeting started and my very real manager and I set off working. Working remotely and communicating remotely is not harder, or more complex than any other job, it's just different.

The same can be said for landing a remote job. The job application is not harder, it's just a bit different. If you immerse yourself in the remote community and show passion for your work, you are sure to separate yourself from other remote job seekers.

How to Be A Happy and Successful Remote Worker?

1. Prioritize purpose in your work

When working remotely, it is even more important to derive meaning from your job since you're missing the camaraderie and personal contact that can give you purpose. No matter what your job is, whether in marketing, engineering, or technical support, there are always ways to find purpose in your work. Think about who is ultimately benefiting from your efforts. Perhaps you helped a customer solve their issue or wrote a useful article. Work is no longer the means to an end, and intrinsic motivators are more powerful today than ever before.

Employers play an important role in helping remote workers feel recognized, too. Once, when I reached the substantial goal of launching a new website, my boss called me to say how happy he was with the end result. He shared how my contribution had played a large role in its success. He said that since he knew I was not in the office, I might not pick up on all the excitement and positive comments the marketing team was getting, so he wanted to call me to tell me himself. As you can imagine, this made me feel very appreciated.

Need more inspiration? Purpose expert Zach Mercurio shares ways to discover purpose while working remotely in 3 Proven Ways to Discover Purpose When You Have a Home Business.

2. Be clear on expectations

Make sure you understand what is expected from you, and take the initiative instead of just waiting for your manager. After finishing a meeting, it's a good idea to follow up with an email and sum up what actions you'll take or provide a summary of the assignment. It's always better to err on the side of being too specific; since you're working remotely, some things may be interpreted differently than you intended. By being more specific, you can avoid miscommunication.

3. Communicate progress

Make it easy for others to see your progress on agreed-upon tasks. According to TalentLMS's remote work statistics survey, the most popular collaborative tools were Skype and Dropbox. These tools, and others like Slack, make it easier for your remote team manager and colleagues to receive an update on your progress whenever they need it.

4. Have regularly scheduled online meetings

If you're working on a project with other team members, it's important to have regularly scheduled meetings. This creates opportunities to talk with team members about items that otherwise wouldn't come up.

5. Meet in person at regular intervals

Even though you can be very effective working remotely, it is important to meet the team in person every now and then. It is much easier to get to know your colleagues on a personal level when meeting face-to-face, which helps you better understand team dynamics. Whether once a month, quarter, or half-year, it's useful to have a regular cadence of visitation with your team. In this way, everyone knows what to expect, and certain activities can be planned during your visit. If remote workers are in the minority, meeting in the office is usually the best setting. If you have a fully-remote team, an offsite retreat is a great solution.

6. Have a friend in the office

When I started working remotely, I instantly formed a good relationship with a new colleague. He realized that I might be missing out on certain things since I was remote, and he took it upon himself to keep me up to date. For instance, he would let me know if there was any feedback from other departments on our work that I may have missed, and he would share company news discussed in the office that wasn't always shared formally.

If you don't already have strong relationships with coworkers, consider trying something like Quuu's weekly buddy system, which has had a significant impact on their team's productivity and happiness.

7. Take regular breaks

Since you'll likely have fewer distractions as a remote worker, you can end up sitting at your desk too long. Get up every hour, grab some fresh air, and set an alarm at the end of the day to avoid working too long. Make sure you get enough physical activity too. Read up on the different ways to avoid being too sedentary.

8.   Designate a separate workspace

Preferably this is a separate room, coworking space, or favorite coffee shop. It's important to have your own space where you can work without distraction when family members or roommates come home. Separating business and personal space can also help put you in a better mindset for getting work done.

9. Combat loneliness

It's easy to feel some loneliness when working alone all day. To combat this, I like to listen to NPR radio. I have the radio on in my living room but away from my main workspace. Then, when I take a break or have my lunch, I listen to the news and discussions, which makes me feel engaged as a remote worker. In addition, I actively seek out social contact, not only with family members but also with other members of the community.

Think about using a coworking space and signing up for meetup.com to see if there are any interesting groups you can join. Book clubs, hiking groups, and professional groups are all great opportunities to meet people while doing the things you love. If you don't see a group you like, you can always start your own.

10.   Have a routine, but be flexible

A great perk of remote work is your flexibility. This means that if evenings or weekends work better for you, you can take advantage of that. However, it's helpful to have a routine and work at set times. That will also make it much easier for your colleagues to collaborate with you.

Working From Home In 2020

Working From Home In 2020

www.ingramcontent.com/pod-product-compliance
Lightning Source LLC
Chambersburg PA
CBHW030514220526
45464CB00006B/2794